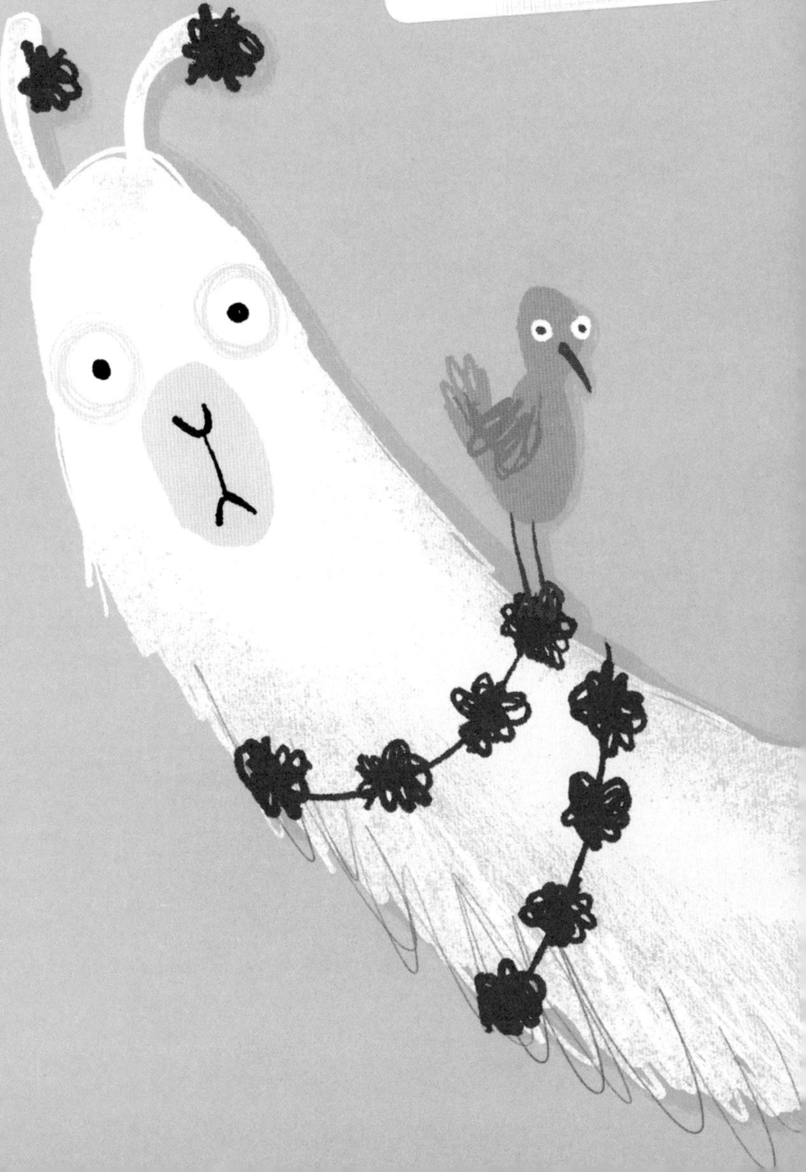

NO DRAMA LLAMA

DROP THE DRAMA AND START LEADING A NO-NONSENSE LIFESTYLE

Sarah Jackson

DOG 'n' BONE

Published in 2019 by Dog 'n' Bone Books
An imprint of Ryland Peters & Small Ltd
20-21 Jockey's Fields   341 E 116th St
London WC1R 4BW   New York, NY 10029

www.rylandpeters.com

10 9 8 7 6 5 4 3 2

Text © Sarah Jackson 2019
Design and illustration © Dog 'n' Bone Books 2019

A CIP catalog record for this book is
available from the Library of Congress
and the British Library.

ISBN: 978 1 912983 01 8

Printed in China

Illustration and design: Sarah Jackson

CONTENTS

INTRODUCTION

Hi! I'm Leroy.

I'm the no drama llama who is going to help you to remove negative tension from your life and encourage you to live a hassle-free existence. Does that sound good? Then keep reading while I fill you in on my background.

I was reared on the arid plains of the Patagonian desert in South America. I learned to survive the harsh climate and tough conditions, and I sure as heck didn't tough it out by moaning my way through life.

TOODLE PIP!

Once I had reached adulthood, I decided I wanted to broaden my horizons, so I left the safety of my herd to see the world.

5

And what an eyeopener that was! I went to some amazing places and tried some new experiences that I never knew existed.

While on my travels, what I realized was how EASY
you humans have it. Fast food, central heating, public
transport, home entertainment, convenience stores...
You name it, you've got it! I also realized you don't know
just how lucky you are. Life couldn't be easier for humans;
you shouldn't have a care in the world. BUT, it seems there
are some of you who aren't content with living the easy
life. Instead, you insist on creating a bit of drama and
making things more difficult than they need to be.

7

SO WHAT'S THE PROBLEM WITH DRAMA?

Let's not confuse what we mean by "drama." We're not talking about a trip to the theater to watch a bit of Shakespeare, oh no! I have plenty of respect for the arts, but let's keep the theatrics on the stage, where they belong.

When I say we should cut the am-dram, I'm talking about those folks who can't resist creating a scene (not the theatrical kind) at every available opportunity.

You know the type, that person who overreacts to everything and has to make a big fuss over the tiniest thing. He or she will often attempt to drag other people into this chaos in the hope of gaining attention and making their own life feel more exciting.

Hands up anyone who knows a few people like this. I thought so.

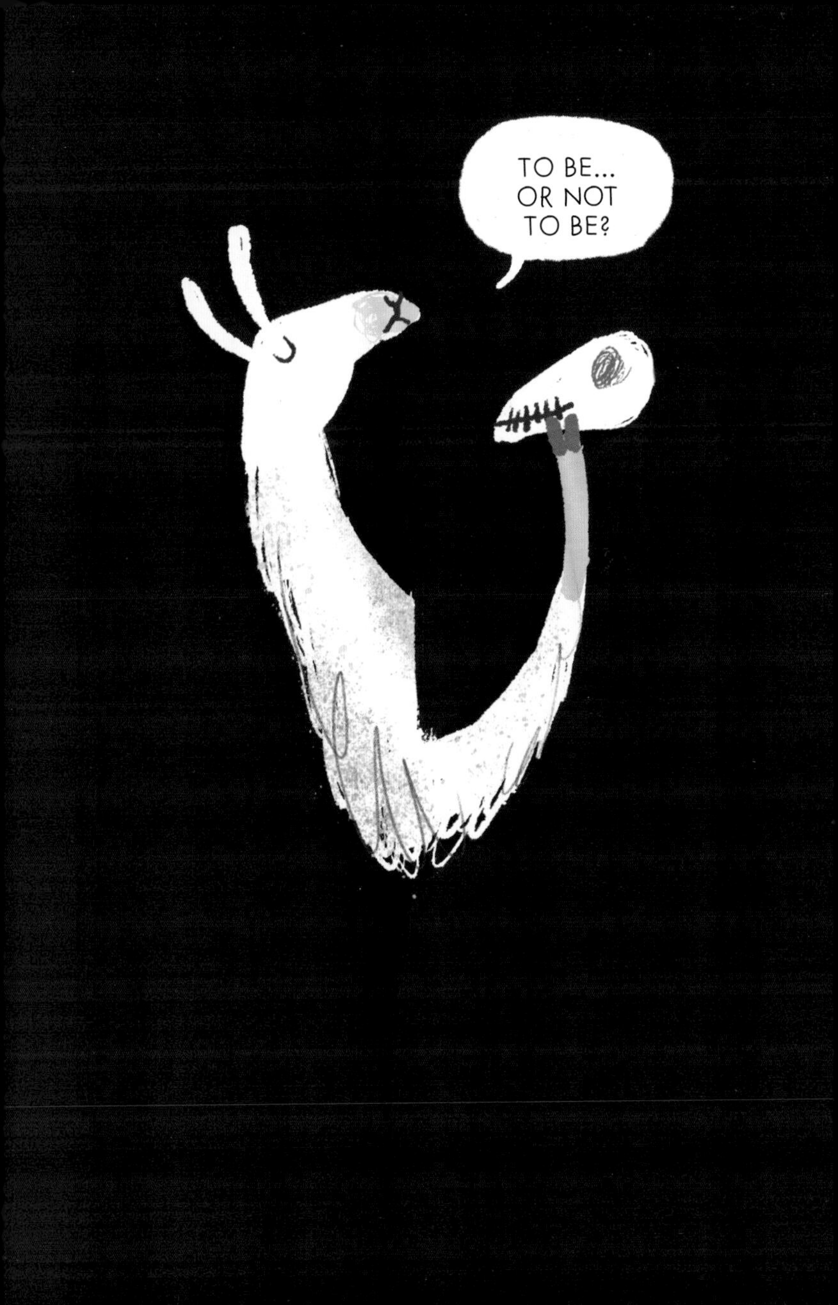
TO BE... OR NOT TO BE?

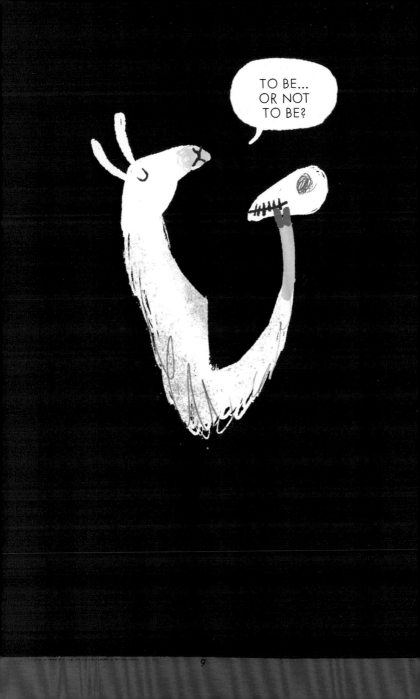

HOW TO SPOT A DRAMA QUEEN

Drama queens come in all shapes and sizes, which means you can't spot one just by looking at him or her. It's generally easier to notice a drama queen when they open their mouths and start talking. In fact, it's rare to find one being quiet in the first place because they just love the sound of their own voice. To help you, here are some telltale warning signs you should look out for:

1. CONSTANTLY GOING ON AND ON AND ON (AND ON) ABOUT ONE'S PROBLEMS.

2. MAKING UP "REAL LIFE" EVENTS THAT SEEM VERY FAR-FETCHED.

3. EXTREME AND INTENSE EMOTIONAL REACTIONS TO MINOR EVENTS OR SITUATIONS. ALSO KNOWN AS "HAVING A TENDENCY TO OVERREACT."

You may say, "What's the harm with the odd bit of drama?" Well, let me tell you.

THE NEGATIVE EFFECTS OF DRAMA

1. ELEVATED STRESS LEVELS

Creating chaos for the sake of it isn't fun for anyone involved. It makes ordinary situations more stressful, which can result in anxiety and raised blood pressure. Not cool, particularly when you're trying to relax and have a nice time.

ARE YOU SURE YOU WANT TO SIT ON THAT BRANCH? IT'S JUST THAT IT LOOKS QUITE FLIMSY AND MIGHT BREAK. I HEARD THROUGH A FRIEND OF A FRIEND ABOUT A BABOON WHO FELL OUT OF THAT TREE LAST WEEK AND LANDED ON A PORCUPINE. IT WASN'T PRETTY, LET ME TELL YOU.

YOUR FACE HAS GONE
VERY RED. YOU SHOULD
GET THAT LOOKED AT.

2. A DECLINE IN POPULARITY

You may have heard of the saying, "Stop making mountains out of molehills." Well, this phrase didn't come out of thin air; those moles are always making a big deal out of nothing. As a result, people have got sick of being around moles and they have become loners. Don't believe me? Think about the last time you saw a mole surrounded by friends... Exactly.

I KNOW THE OTHER MOLES HAVE BEEN TALKING ABOUT ME. I MAY BE NEARLY BLIND, BUT I'M NOT DEAF.

THANKFULLY I AM DEAF. SO I DON'T HAVE TO LISTEN TO HIM.

To help illustrate the importance of this point, I've drawn a handy graph that shows the relationship between the amount of drama and the number of friends.

NOTE: Having loads of friends can add unnecessary drama to your life, so it's best not to have too many, anyway. More on that later.

3. LOSS OF REALITY

Some folk can even get so caught up in their own dramas that they actually lose touch with reality and their heads become filled with wild delusions.

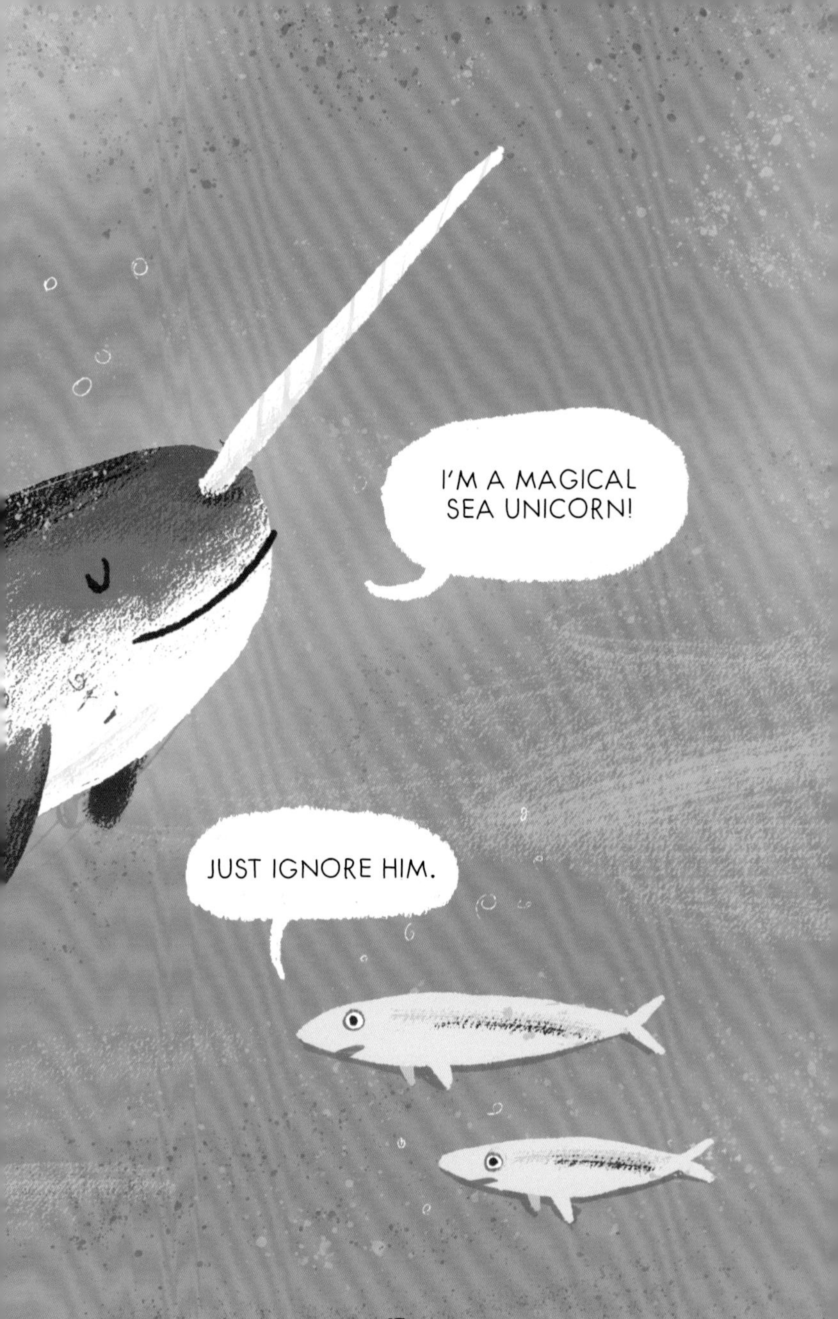
I'M A MAGICAL SEA UNICORN!
JUST IGNORE HIM.

This isn't just a modern-day phenomena. Drama queens have been around since the dawn of civilization...

UGH!
I JUST <u>CAN'T</u> DO THIS ANYMORE. IT'S GOING TO TAKE <u>AGES</u> AND I'M SO <u>TIRED</u>!

I HATE MY LIFE.

MAYBE IF HE HAD JUST GOT ON WITH THE JOB THEN IT WOULDN'T HAVE TAKEN SO LONG. ISN'T THAT RIGHT, BOB?

And even before that.

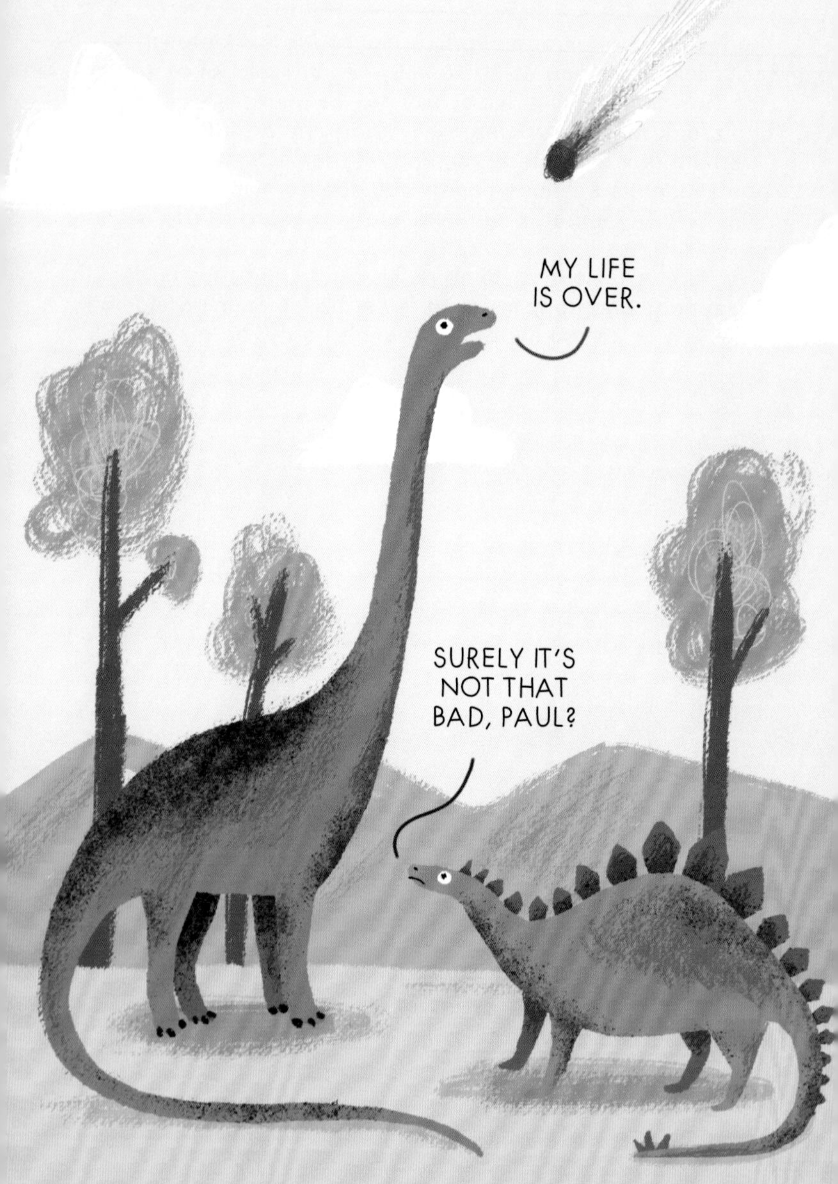
MY LIFE
IS OVER.
SURELY IT'S
NOT THAT
BAD, PAUL?

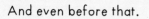

So I'm here with this important message for all those drama queens out there:

Some of us just want to go quietly about our day and have a pleasant time without having to listen to other people's minor crises, moaning, and nonsense!

That's why I decided to become a life coach. Alongside that I have set up a campaign, with the help of my family and friends, to stop drama queens in their tracks.

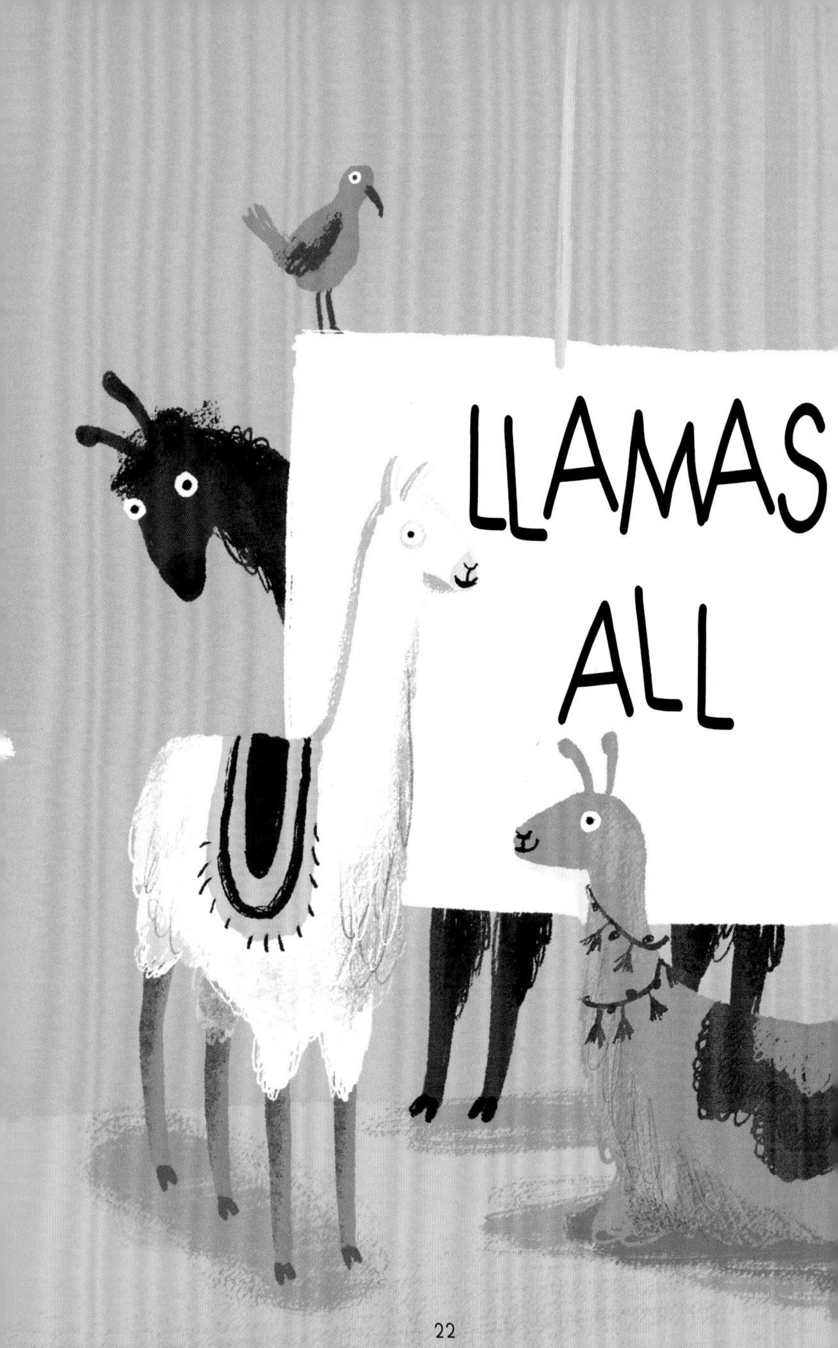
LLAMAS
ALL

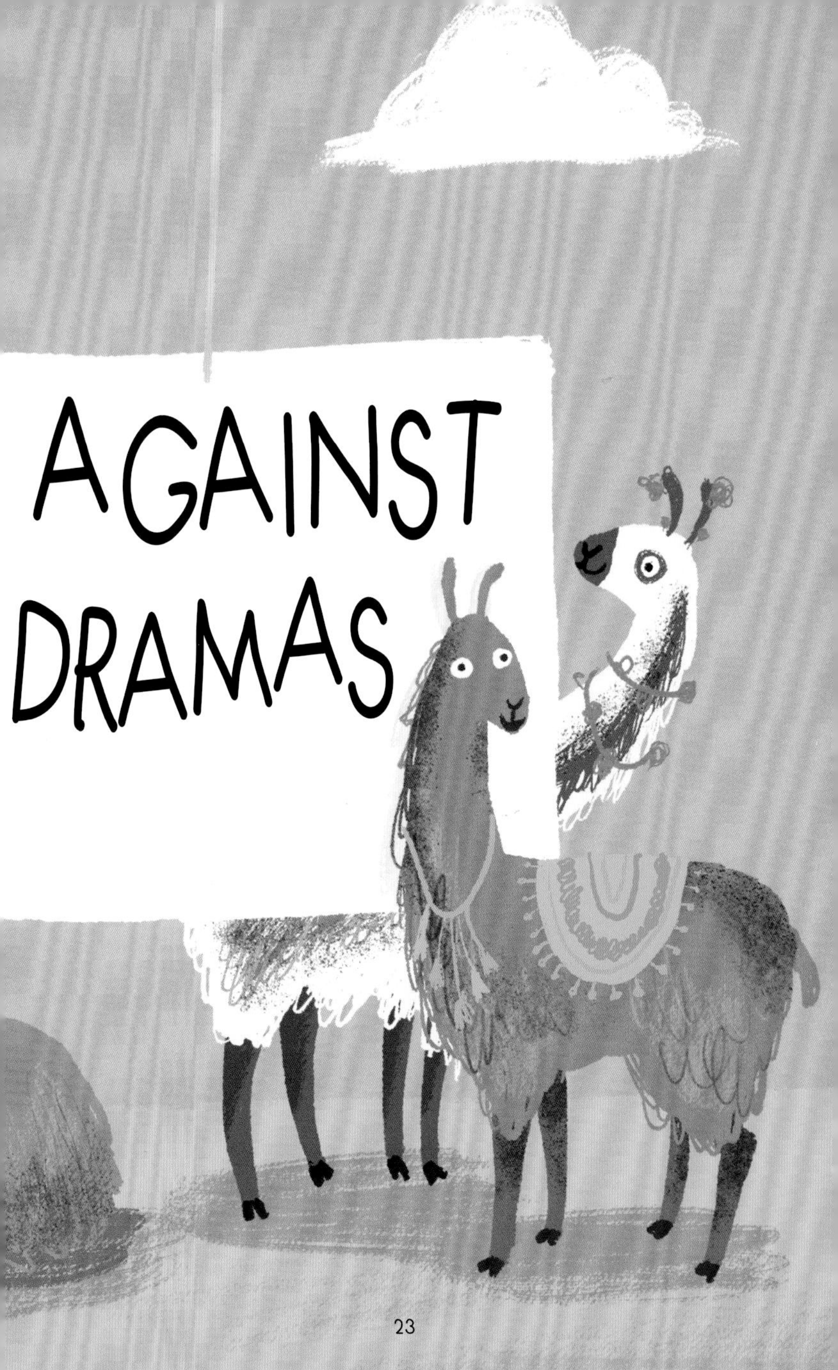
AGAINST
DRAMAS

You may have been wondering who this bird is?

Well, he's my secretary, Bob.

Some people have questioned whether in this day and age it's still OK to call Bob's species a secretary bird. I checked with Bob if he'd rather change his name to personal assistant bird, but he said it was fine, so no drama. Phew. Bob's old school, you see. He even still uses a typewriter.

I'm occasionally asked why a llama needs a secretary. I usually tell them to mind their own business.

Since becoming rather well-known in the life-coaching industry, I receive a lot of letters from fans requesting advice and tips on how they can become more like me. Unfortunately, I can't spend all day replying to this fan mail. To get round this, Bob reads the letters first and then passes over the good ones for me to have a read through.

He also files my tax returns, speaks to my mother for me once every week, and sometimes does my grocery shopping. Bob takes care of all the things that could potentially add unnecessary discord to my life. And he loves it, don't you Bob?

...

Don't worry about him. He's shy.

WHERE TO SPOT A DRAMA QUEEN

So, now you know all about drama queens and the negative effects they can have on your life, the next question on your lips is probably...

"How do I avoid them?"

Great question. In order to work out how to dodge drama, I had to go looking for it. I spent a few years doing some important detective work, conducting extensive field research into this matter. As a result of my investigation, I have come to the following conclusion...

Drama can be created almost anywhere!

However, over the next few pages I have highlighted the main areas of your life where drama can be found.

THAT PLACE LOOKS VERY SUSPICIOUS TO ME, BOB.

1. FAMILY

You can't choose your family. And if you've ever watched a TV soap opera then you know that family emergencies are as common as rats in the subway.

As I may have previously mentioned, we llamas really hate dramas. Therefore, when it comes to relatives we all try our best to get along without rubbing each other up the wrong way. However, if you're not lucky enough to have a fuss-free family then your options are limited.

It is possible to divorce members of your family, but I've been told it's time consuming, expensive, and, if you ask me, a touch melodramatic!

MY ADVICE: Use earplugs, that way you don't have to listen to any grousing. If you don't have any to hand, then improvise!

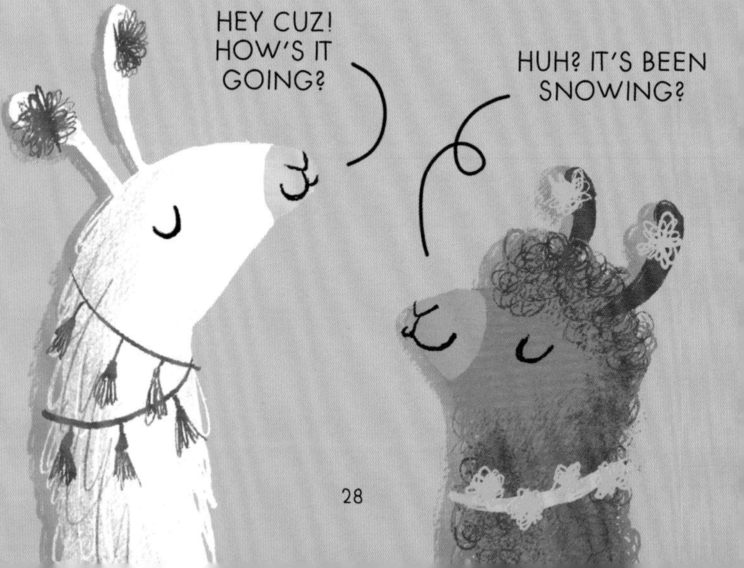
HEY CUZ! HOW'S IT GOING?
HUH? IT'S BEEN SNOWING?

2. FRIENDS

Unlike family, you can choose your friends, so if you've buddied up with a drama queen then you've really only got yourself to blame!

When on the look out for some new companions, then it's worth looking out for a few of the signs that I mentioned earlier. Alternatively, why not subject them to a personality test that will help determine whether or not they are going to be the fuss-free type of friend that you're looking for.

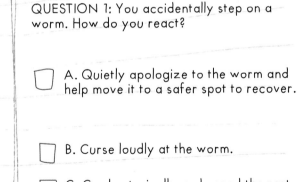

QUESTION 1: You accidentally step on a worm. How do you react?

☐ A. Quietly apologize to the worm and help move it to a safer spot to recover.

☐ B. Curse loudly at the worm.

☐ C. Cry hysterically and spend the rest of your day trying to find the victim's next of kin.

☐ D. It wasn't an accident.

3. RELATIONSHIPS

Over the years, I've lost count of the number of stories I've heard about relationship dramas and woes. If you aren't lucky enough to find that special someone who "gets" you, then you may find yourself falling into one of these common relationship pitfalls...

TOO CLINGY

ARGUMENTATIVE

TOO JEALOUS

IT'S COMPLICATED

I met one chap on my travels who had at least eight wives, and he never got a moment's peace. They were constantly in his ear hole, droning on endlessly about trifling matters that really weren't important. Unsurprisingly, the poor guy was constantly bad tempered and grumpy.

WHY HAVEN'T YOU
DONE THE WASHING UP?

MY ADVICE: If you really want to save yourself some trouble and strife, then I suggest you fly solo and spend more quality time with number one... that's you!

4. WORK

The workplace is constantly filled with drama and it's not hard to see why. Throw together a bunch of people for eight hours a day who have nothing in common except for the coffee machine they drink from and you've a recipe for dramatic disaster.

Gossiping, backstabbing, trash-talking, and constant complaining are commonplace from the office drama queens. They can make the day a miserable slog for those of us who just want to get on with our jobs and clock off on time.

MY ADVICE: Try to distance yourself from the moaners and your coworkers who are determined to create problems where there aren't any. They'll only put a dampener on your day.

I'M SICK OF THAT QUEEN BEE ALWAYS TELLING ME WHAT TO DO. WHO DOES SHE THINK SHE IS?

UM. SHE'S YOUR BOSS, KAREN.

As well as the moaners, you've also got the show-offs who always HAVE to be the center of attention. Not content just getting on with their work, they spend most of the time telling everyone how good they are at their job, rather than actually being good at it.

TELL-TALE SIGN: Look out for the person who goes way over the top "dressing to impress"—the one who is often found posing anywhere in the office apart from at their own desk.

I THOUGHT IT WAS DRESS <u>DOWN</u> DAY?!

5. BODY IMAGE

This planet is full of shallow beings who are focused on looks. Sadly, we can't all be gifted with the long, slender limbs and luscious locks us llamas are blessed with...
But that's not the point.

Drama queens are particularly bad at only concentrating on the superficial things in life and making an enormous deal out of them.

MY NEW HAIR STRAIGHTENERS AREN'T WORKING. I CAN'T GO OUT LIKE THIS.

DOES THIS NEW HAIRCUT MAKE MY NOSE LOOK BIG? I THINK IT DOES. MAYBE I SHOULD GET A NEW NOSE?

I'd like to tell you a little story about the "Ugly Duckling." Some of you might have heard it before, so I'll make it quick.

Basically, a duck had some babies and one of them was not the same as the other cute yellow fluffy ducklings. Instead, he was scruffy and gray and made a big fuss about being different and not fitting in. The duckling lived in solitude for most of his life because he was embarrassed about the way he looked.

One day, when out swimming by himself, the duckling met some swans who invited him to hang out with them. He couldn't understand why they would want to do that until he saw his reflection and realized he'd turned into a handsome swan himself.

That's a MASSIVE overreaction if you ask me, Bob! Instead of going off in a big sulk and crying like a baby, he could've instead got on with things and saved himself all that heartache.

OH, CRY ME A RIVER, MATE.

I HAVE.

6. FASHION

The world of fashion is a crazy one and it can get people ever so stressed out. With preening prima donnas spending all sorts of money following the latest fads and trends (and often getting it wrong), it's easy to see why some fashion victims get a little carried away. Not to mention the fact that your outfit choices can be scrutinized all over cyberspace, thanks to Twitter, Snapchat, and all that malarkey.

MY ADVICE: Don't let it bother you. Clothes are there to keep you warm and your private bits covered! Who cares how they look? Us llamas are known for being rather experimental, choosing different styles and snazzy color, and we don't care if it's not to everyone else's taste.

Here are some of my favorite looks I've tested out over the years...

Camo-llama

Pompoms and a perm, a classic look!

Hippie... Peace and llamas, man!

Rock 'n' roll

This was just a curtain that I found. It's a great look for formal occasions; just look at those tassels!

37

7. LIFE'S BIG QUESTIONS

Sometimes we can cause unnecessary stress and anxiety by worrying about things that are outside of our control. Some people spend too much time concerned about life's big questions, such as...

I can't answer those questions!

If you ask me it's pointless getting all worked up about finding the answers. What does it matter anyway?!

MY ADVICE: If you're not good with decisions, stop making a fuss about inconsequentialities and focus instead on solving real-life everyday dilemmas.

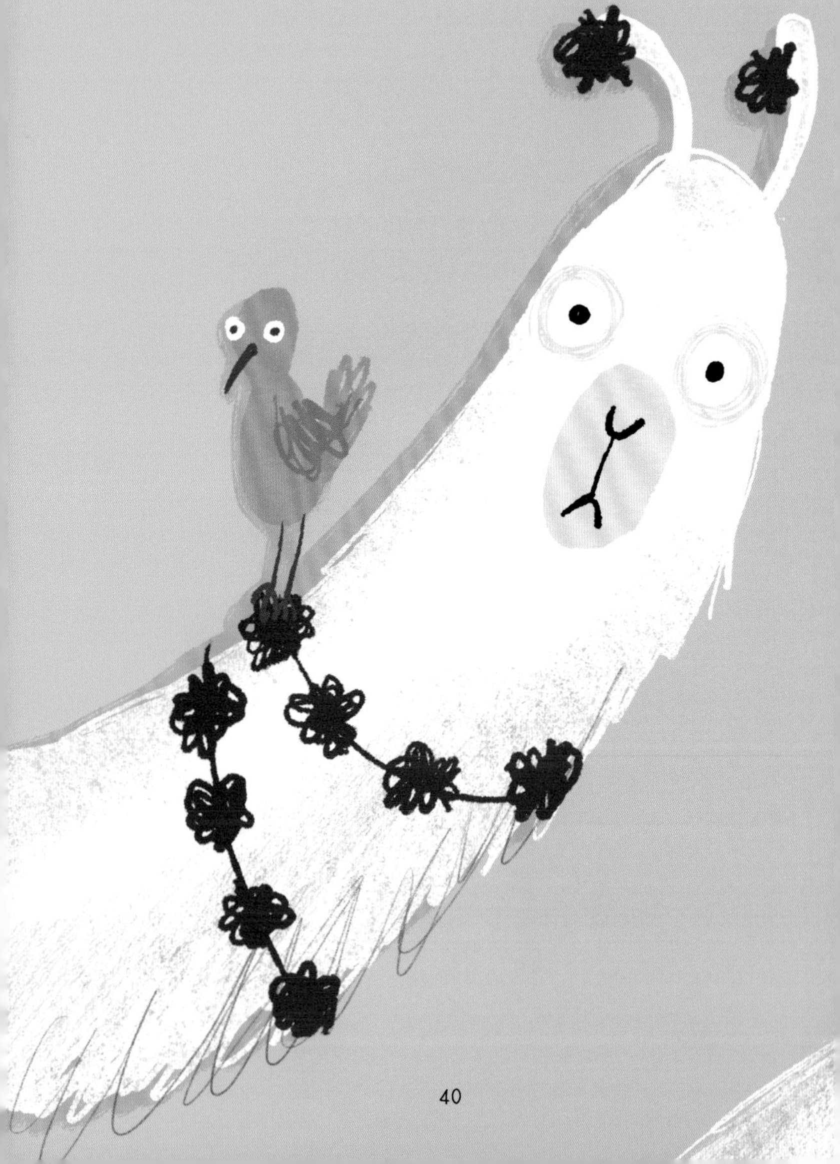

It's time to put a stop to this nonsense! Luckily for you, I'm going to tell you how.

(And yes, those are pompoms on my stop sign. Thank you for noticing!)

41

HOW TO KICK DRAMA IN THE BUTT

Now that we've learned how to identify a drama queen and where the most common sources of drama can be found, what can we do to deal with it? This is where my life-coaching techniques will become invaluable to you. These practical steps will help you kick unwanted drama in the butt... FOR GOOD!

Before we get started, I'd like to get you practicing this visualization technique that should really help focus your mind, as demonstrated here by Bob and this helpful volunteer...

OK BOB, IMAGINE THIS
HIPPO REPRESENTS
DRAMA. NOW...

KICK IT
IN THE BUTT!

NOTE: This exercise is for visualization purposes only. Please don't go around kicking hippos in the butt. It will make them very angry.

1. GET TOUGH

Drama queens don't respond well to subtlety–they simply don't understand it! In order to snap them out of their state of self-importance and melodrama you need to get tough with them. You have to let them know, in no uncertain terms, that you aren't interested in their petty problems and that they should take their grievances elsewhere. Be polite, but be firm.

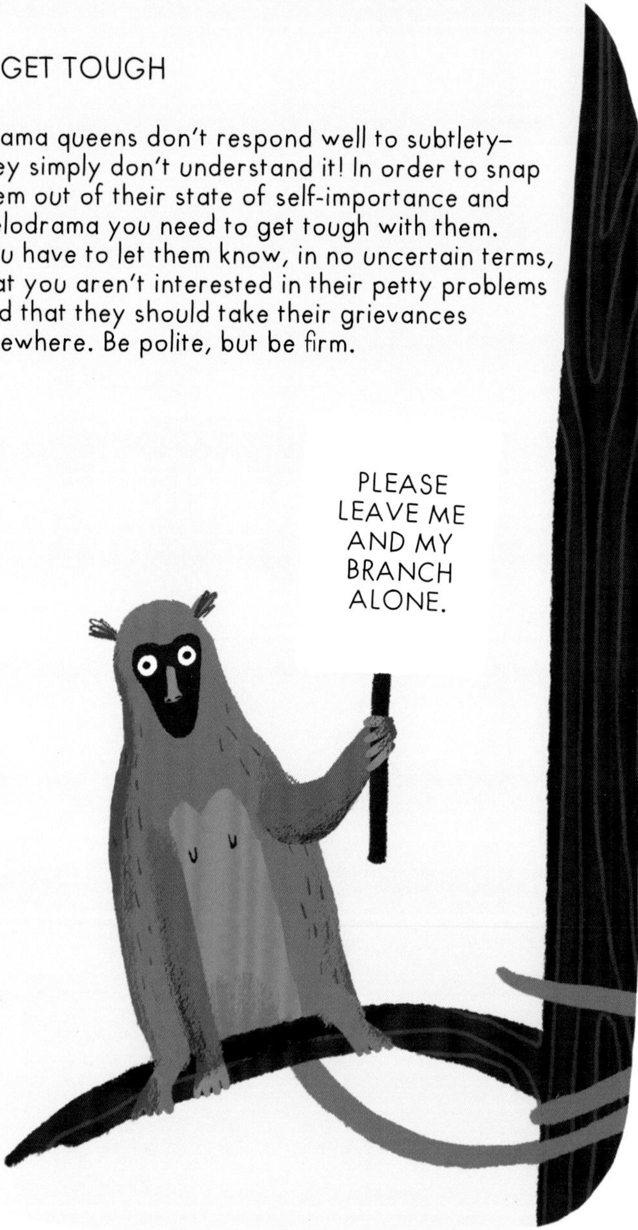
PLEASE
LEAVE ME
AND MY
BRANCH
ALONE.

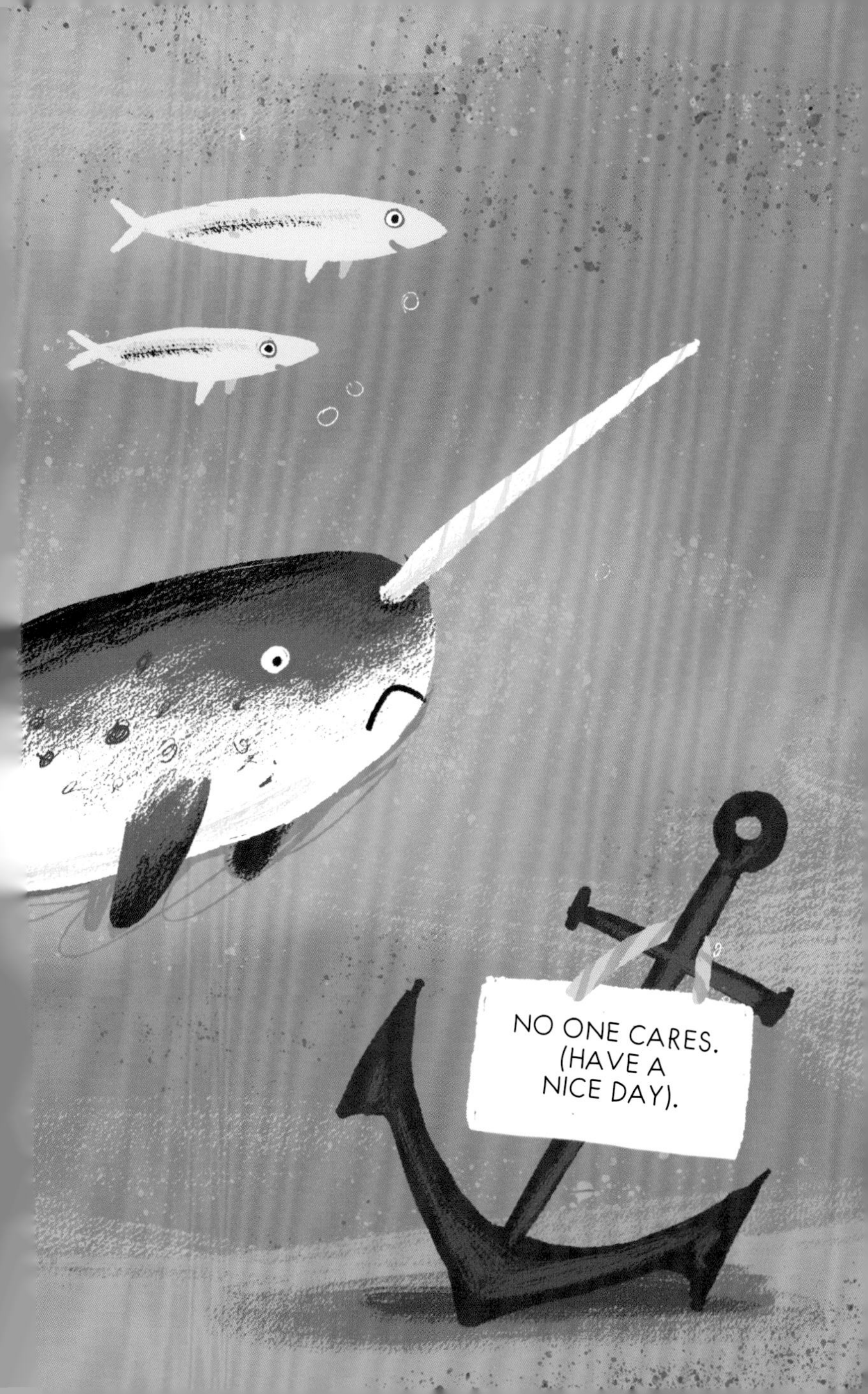
NO ONE CARES.
(HAVE A
NICE DAY).

2. CREATE A BUBBLE

The greatest defense you can have against others is the ability to just let things wash over you and not care. There are lots of techniques you can learn that will help with this, from meditation and positivity mantras to mindfulness and deep breathing. These techniques could give you all the tools you need to block out other people's bellyaches and allow you to focus on your own inner peace.

I met a great guy called Brian on my travels. He has completely mastered the art of meditation and spends 23 hours a day in a relaxed meditative state.

Of course, mastering the art of metaphorical bubble creation can take years, and sometimes decades of practice to perfect. Furthermore, self-improvement doesn't actually stop those drama queens in their tracks, it just makes YOU an even better person.

If that all sounds a bit too much like hard work, then you could just buy a large plastic bubble to live in and shut yourself away from everyone.

MY ADVICE: Don't forget air holes!

3. REMOVE TOXIC RELATIONSHIPS

Sometimes that bubble isn't enough to protect you from persistent drama queens who are determined to disturb your peace.

This is where we need to get really tough! If there's a mood hoover you know whose antics are constantly sending you to despair, then maybe it's time to just cut the ties and say, "Farewell to you."

It may sound harsh, but just think of how liberated you will feel not having to listen to their woes, moans, and daily grumbling!

MY ADVICE: Don't feel too bad about it. Your former acquaintance will only give them something else to whinge about, which they'll love!

Some people may argue that it's a bold move to end a relationship all together, but I recently gave this advice to a good pal of mine and he says he's never been happier!

MY ADVICE: It's not a good idea to use insect repellent to call time on a relationship. Instead I advise you to try a brief conversation, voicemail, or text message.

If that fails, then you could always revert to what millennials refer to as "ghosting." Don't worry, it's not as spooky as it sounds. It just involves ignoring fun sponges until they get the hint.

4. ENJOY SOME ALONE TIME

If these techniques haven't helped and you're still feeling a bit worn out by everyone else's theatrics, then it's time you took yourself away from it all. It's time to go off grid!

Take a break, go on a trip, get as far away as possible from everyone you know. I regularly take time out to explore the four corners of the Earth and find some true peace and quiet with only Bob for company.

MY ADVICE: Make sure you leave your phone at home. They'll only try and track you down.

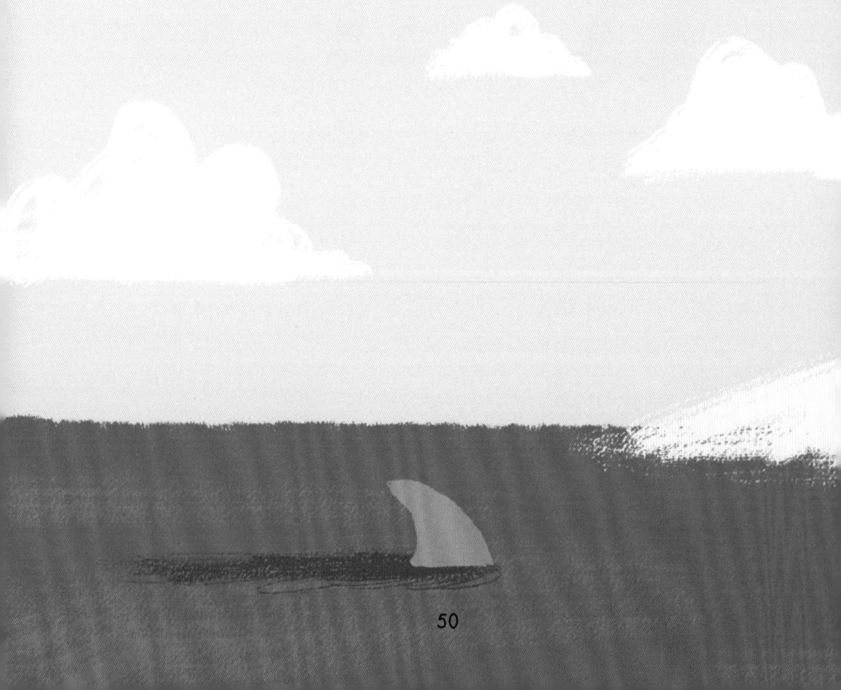

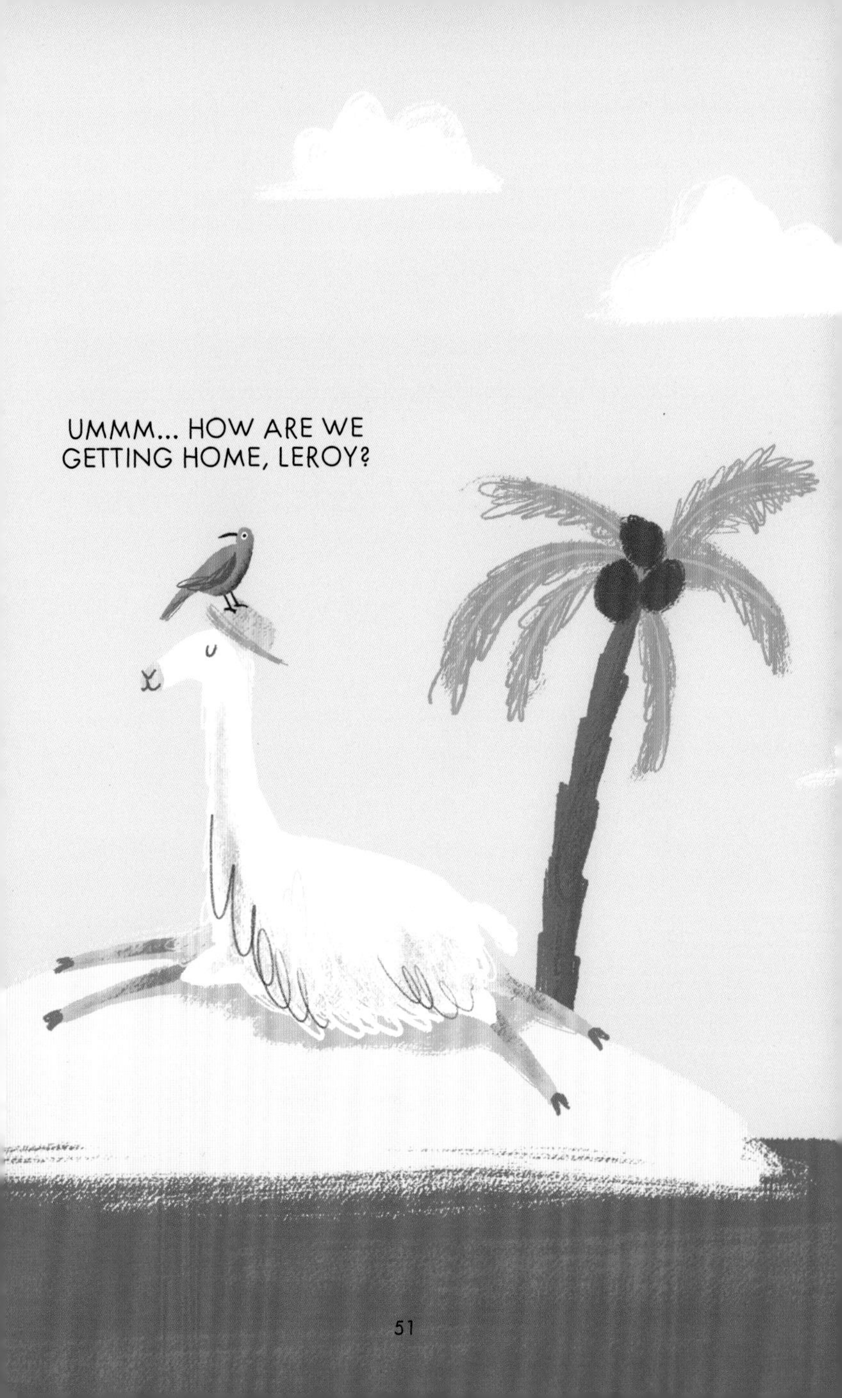
UMMM... HOW ARE WE GETTING HOME, LEROY?

5. DON'T BECOME A DRAMA QUEEN

I've told you how to get drama queens out of your life, but it's even more important to make sure you don't become one yourself. Here are some hints for making sure you stay levelheaded and drama free.

PICK A ROLE MODEL: Think of someone you know who always stays calm and never overreacts to anything that life throws their way. Try to be more like them. My role model is Calvin the Cool Cucumber.

I JUST LOVE
HOW UNFLAPPABLE
YOU ARE, CALVIN.

KEEP THESE HANDY ITEMS WITH YOU AS
PART OF YOUR NO DRAMA TOOL KIT:

Pompoms and safety pins
to prevent emergency
fashion dramas

Eye mask for
pretending to
be asleep

Signs

DRAMA-
FREE
ZONE

I'M NOT
INTERESTED

Role model

Pencil for
writing
more signs

SURROUND YOURSELF WITH
PEOPLE WHO WILL HELP KEEP
YOU GROUNDED:

<u>CALM DOWN, DAVID!</u>
YOU'LL BURST ANOTHER
BLOOD VESSEL.

SPREAD THE WORD!

It's great that you've set out to remove drama from your life, but why stop there?

You don't have to be a llama to join our "llamas against all dramas" campaign, because we are always on the look out for new recruits to share the message. To help with the campaign I've had Bob create some fantastic promotional merchandise...

Slogan signs and posters

THIS HOME IS A DRAMA-FREE ZONE

SAY NO TO THE DRAMA SHOW

KEEP CALM AND SHUT UP!

Wipe-clean placard and pens. Perfect for campaigning and writing your own messages!

Photographic posters featuring yours truly and Bob.

BE MORE
BOB!

T-shirts, available
in all sizes.

Keyrings

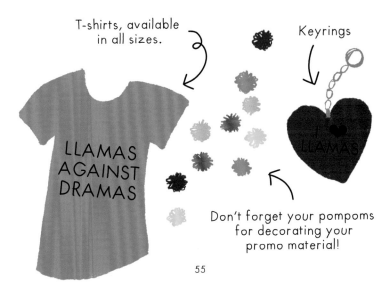

LLAMAS
AGAINST
DRAMAS

Don't forget your pompoms
for decorating your
promo material!

Since becoming a life coach, I like to offer free, impartial advice to those out there who are struggling with dramas... Be it other people's or their own.

I'd like to share some of my favorite letters that some of you readers will possibly be able to relate to, alongside my helpful responses.

Dear Leroy,

I've been experiencing some bullying in the workplace and don't know what to do. I enjoy my job, but none of my coworkers want to sit next to me and they avoid spending time with me in the break room. Last week I returned to my desk to find a selection of air fresheners and an antiperspirant with a note that read "use me." What's their problem?!

Yours sincerely,

Eric

Well Eric, what a bunch of drama queens! It's clear that you have an issue with emitting bodily odors in the office and your colleagues have some kind of problem with this. I would say you have two options:

1. Use the antiperspirants and hope that your smell is rather more appealing to co-workers.

2. Don't bother with them. It sounds like they're making a big song and dance about a bit of whiff. Be proud of who you are and whatever smells you make!

Warmest whiffs (I mean wishes),

Leroy

Hi Leroy,

I'm 46 and I still live with my mother. I'm so bored.
All my friends are boring and the same is true of
everyone in my family. I spend all my time reading
gossip magazines because I think that celebrities
are more interesting
than anybody I know
in real life.

I wish that something
exciting would
happen to me,
but I don't have
any money because
I don't have
a job. I also blew
all my cash on the
magazines. What
should I do?

Marjorie

Hi Marjorie,

Maybe you should look at whether it's the world around
you that is boring, or whether it's actually you who is the
dull one. You should also get a job.

Leroy

Hi Leroy,

My brother is constantly making up stories that aren't
true. When it's just the two of us, he's his normal self.
However, as soon as other people are around it's like
he becomes a different person, full of tall tales and
white lies told in order to be the center of attention.
I don't know why he acts this way. It's annoying
and I wish he would stop it. Do you have any advice?

Thanks in advance.

Peter

Hi Peter,

It seems to me like your brother is perhaps suffering from
some low self-esteem. It's likely that he is trying to impress
those around him by inventing stories that make him sound
more exciting to them.

You could try reassuring him, explaining that he's great
as he his and doesn't need the bravado to make friends.
Or you could tell him that no one cares and that he should
stop showing off.

Good luck!

Leroy

Hi Leroy,

I'm really concerned about aliens. I'm convinced that I'm being watched by extraterrestrials from another galaxy and that they are trying to infiltrate my brain.

When I speak to friends about this they laugh at me and tell me I'm being over dramatic. They say I should forget about it, but I know that they've been brainwashed to come out with that. I feel like the whole world has been overtaken by these aliens and that none of us are safe anymore. I'm writing to you as I think you might be the only person that I can trust. I want to warn you that I think your assistant Bob has been possessed by the aliens and that you should stop seeing him.

I hope this letter finds you in time and that you can reply to me before it's too late.

Stuart

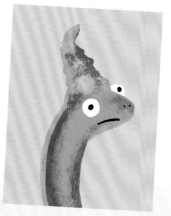

Dear Stuart,

Firstly let me commend you on that rather jazzy tin foil hat! Secondly, I think you should seek professional help.

Best of luck!

Leroy

And to everyone who's written to me for some life coaching, please be reassured that Bob reads every letter which comes our way. If you don't get a reply it's because your problem is not worth my time and you should just get a grip.

Bob and I would like to say thank you for taking the time to read this book, and as a result helping the world become a quieter, less dramatic place to be!

We hope that you are able to use the advice in this book to help "kick drama in the butt" and go about your day in peace!

GRAZIE!

DANKE!

ARIGATO!

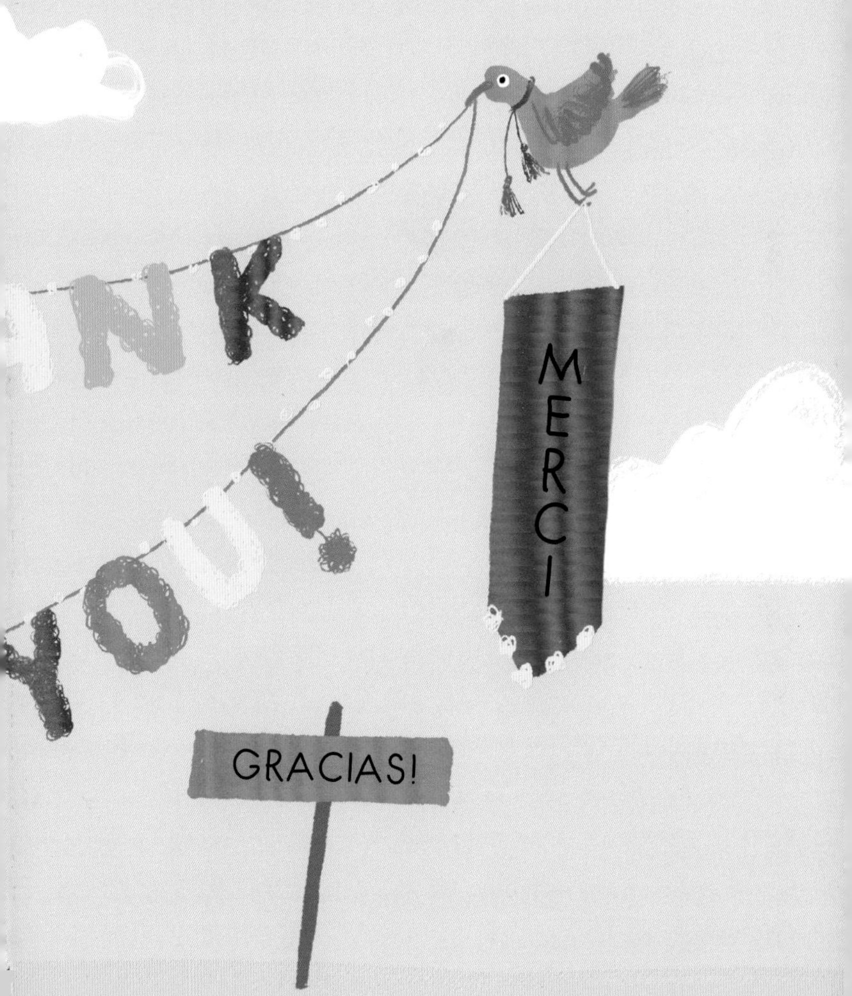
NK
YOU!
MERCI
GRACIAS!

ACKNOWLEDGMENTS

I'd like to thank my family and friends for being level-headed llamas and not all about the dramas.

This book is dedicated to my Nana, Pat, who demanded I write a book about alpacas (hopefully this is close enough).

OUCH!

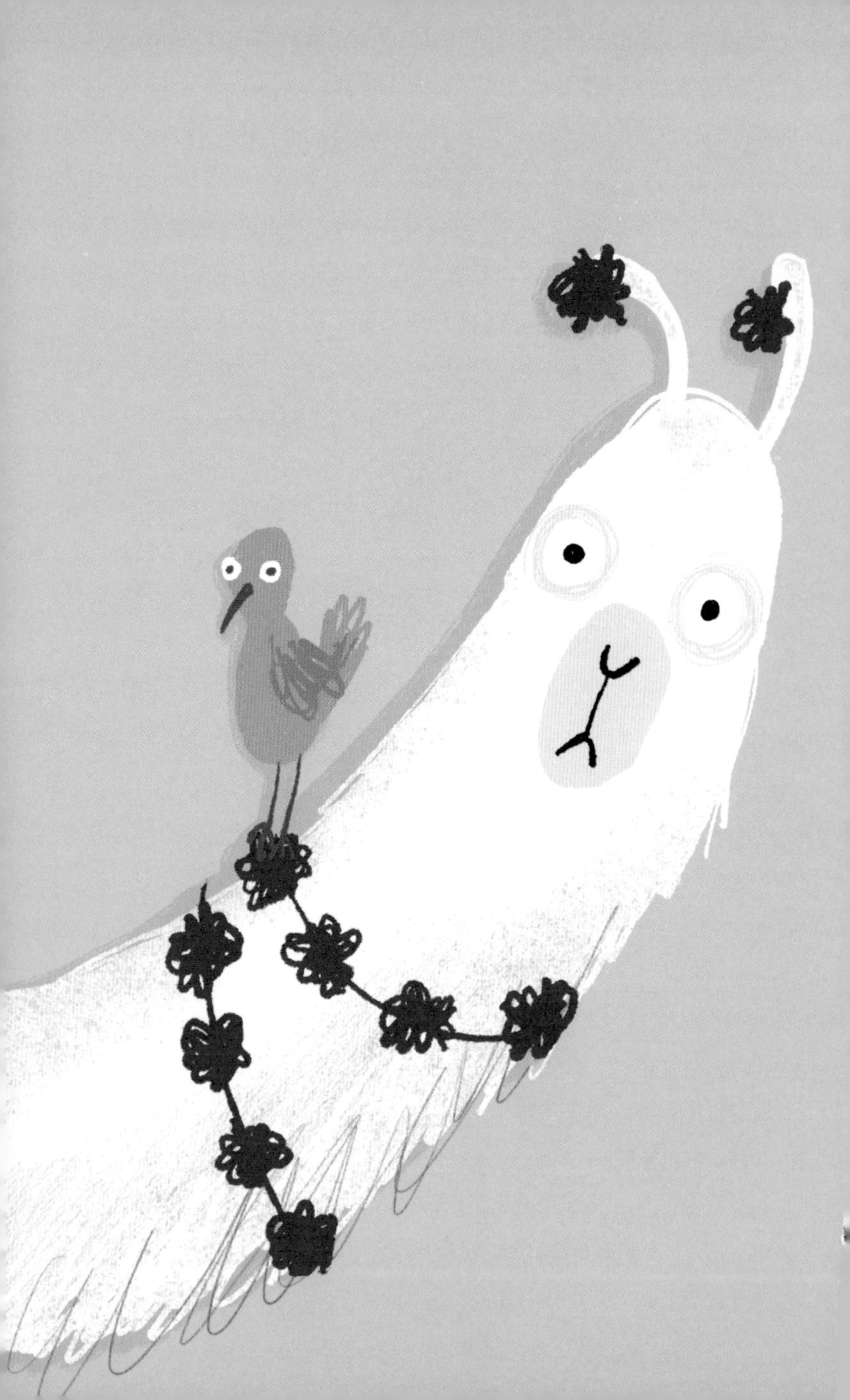